SCIENCE IN OUR WORLD

WATER

J551·48

Contributory Author
Brian Knapp, BSc, PhD
Art Director
Duncan McCrae
Special photography
Graham Servante
Special models
Tim Fulford, Head of CDT, Leighton Park School
Editorial consultants
Anna Grayson, Rita Owen
Science advisor
Jack Brettle, BSc, PhD, Chief Research Scientist,
Pilkington plc
Environmental Education Advisor
Colin Harris, County Advisor, Herts. CC
Illustrators
Tim Smith and Mark Franklin
Production controller
Gillian Gatehouse
Print consultants
Landmark Production Consultants Ltd
Printed and bound in Hong Kong

Designed and produced by EARTHSCAPE EDITIONS,

First published in the United Kingdom in 1991
by Atlantic Europe Publishing Company Ltd,
86 Peppard Road, Sonning Common, Reading,
Berkshire, RG4 9RP

Copyright © 1991
Atlantic Europe Publishing Company Ltd

British Library Cataloguing in Publication Data

Knapp, Brian
  Water
  1. Water – For children
  I. Title   II. Series
  553.7

ISBN 1-869860-60-8

In this book you will find some words that have been shown in **bold** type. There is a full explanation of each of these words on pages 46 and 47.

On many pages you will find experiments that you might like to try for yourself. They have been put in a coloured box like this.

6736

Acknowledgements
The publishers would like to thank the following:
Martin Morris, Stephen Pitcher, Leighton Park
School, Micklands County Primary School,
Redlands County Primary School

Picture credits
t=top b= bottom l=left r=right

All photographs from the Earthscape Editions
photographic library except the following:
Adam Hart-Davis 38b; Bruce Coleman 32t, 37t;
Colin Garratt 44; ZEFA 4, 11, 28b, 29b, 41b

Contents

Introduction

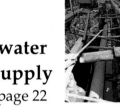

Look out of the window. The clouds in the sky are tiny droplets of water waiting to fall as rain. Turn on a tap. Clean water comes gushing out. We use water for drinking, for cooking, for cleaning, for watering our plants and flushing the toilet. We use water for carrying heavy loads in ships or for carrying heat round our homes – even driving our power stations.

Look at yourself. You are nearly all water; your blood contains a large amount of water. The air you breath out is moist, and even the tear-drops in your eyes are water.

Water is all around us in everything we do, and yet we use such a tiny amount.

steam
page 44

water cycle
page 8

kinds of water
page 6

surface tension
page 38

electric power
page 18

Over nine-tenths of all the world's water lies in the oceans. Most of the rest is locked away as ice on the cold continent of Antarctica surrounding the South Pole or as frozen Arctic seas surrounding the North Pole. A mere one hundredth of the world's water flows in rivers, even though they may look mighty to us.

Too much water or too little water can cause disasters and deaths. In today's world we need to learn how to control rivers, clean water and more importantly still, how to save water.

Discover the fascinating world of water in any way you choose. Just turn to a page and begin your discoveries.

swelling
page 40

hot water
page 42

gas
page 34

grease
page 36

weight
page 16

What is water?

Water is a liquid – you are able to pour it. But look at this 'bowl'; it is made of ice. This too is water but it is a solid.

Leave the solid and the liquid in a bowl and they will both disappear. The liquid and the solid will have become a gas called **water vapour**. Water is so useful in our lives because it can occur in these three different forms: liquid water, solid ice and gas.

An ice bowl being used to pour water

Make a solid, liquid, gas bowl

If you want to make an icy glass that disappears, you need two tall plastic bowls. One bowl should be about a centimetre smaller across and a centimetre less deep than the other. The bigger one should have a lid that clips on.

Put one bowl inside the other and fill the space with water. Hold the inside bowl down while you do this and leave about a centimetre gap at the top. Fit the lid. This will hold the inside bowl down.

Carefully put the bowls in a freezer. Your ice glass can be taken out next day. You can even have a drink from it.

Steam

Boiling point 100°C

All change

Water turns from solid to liquid to gas in jumps. At 0 °C it turns from a solid into a liquid. This temperature is called the melting point. At 100 °C it turns from a liquid into vapour. This temperature is called the boiling point.

Water can be solid or liquid or gas because it is made of millions of tiny particles called **molecules**. If they are very close together they cannot easily move and the water appears as a solid – we call it ice.

When the water is warmer there is more space between the molecules to move about and the result is a liquid – water.

When the molecules are spaced far apart they become invisible. This is water vapour. Steam is tiny water droplets made from cooling vapour.

Liquid water

Freezing point 0°C

Ice

Where water comes from

Moisture cools and
makes cloud droplets

Water turns
to moisture
and rises

On Earth, water is one of the commonest
of all substances and without it life would
be impossible.

It has taken billions of years to fill the
great oceans, but now water covers three
quarters of the earth's surface.

The oceans are the Earth's great water
reservoirs, but huge amounts move into
the skies each day, make clouds and form
rivers. This cycling of water is called the
water cycle.

Water is stored
in the oceans

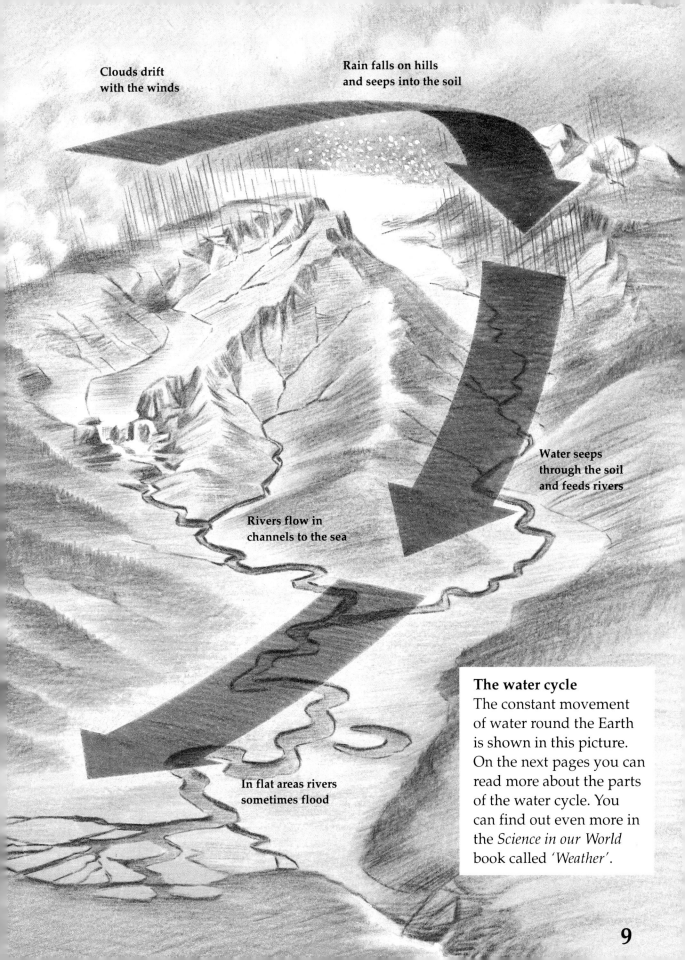

Clouds drift
with the winds

Rain falls on hills
and seeps into the soil

Water seeps
through the soil
and feeds rivers

Rivers flow in
channels to the sea

In flat areas rivers
sometimes flood

The water cycle
The constant movement
of water round the Earth
is shown in this picture.
On the next pages you can
read more about the parts
of the water cycle. You
can find out even more in
the *Science in our World*
book called *'Weather'*.

The salt of the sea

Straw

Sea-water makes up over nine-tenths of all the water in the world. A glass of clean sea-water may look as clear as a glass of tap water. But the salt **dissolved** in sea-water makes it very different to tap water in many ways.

Salt measurer
Water containing dissolved salt is an example of a **solution**.

It is not easy to tell how salty a salt solution is just by looking at it. A simple float can help. Make one from a straw and a ball of Plasticine or Blu-tack as shown here.

The more salt dissolved in the water, the higher the float will ride. You could draw marks on the side of the float and make a scale of saltiness.

Push a rolled ball of Plasticine or Blu-tack on to the end of the straw to act as a stopper and weight

The floating sea

It is much easier to float or swim in the sea than in a swimming pool. The salt dissolved in the water helps to make the water thicker, or more dense, and this makes it harder to sink.

Some inland seas are so salty, or **saline**, that people could never sink in them no matter how hard they might try.

Salty seas and lakes

Seas and lakes near deserts are much saltier than seas and lakes in places where it rains all year. This is because more water is lost as moisture from a hot sea or lake than falls back as rain. In rainy places it is the other way round.

The white 'tide mark' along the shores of this lake is made from salt.

Salt solution

The amount of salt you can dissolve in water may surprise you.

Put a cupful of cold tap water in a clear measuring jug and add a teaspoon of salt. Stir well until the salt goes away. Keep adding salt, half a spoonful at a time until the salt will not go away. Check to see how much salt you have added.

Now ask a grown-up to help you to warm the solution in a saucepan. Pour the warm water back into the jug and see how much more salt you can add.

Let the water cool and see what happens.

From rain to rivers

Although rain can do little to change the landscape, when it gathers together as a river it becomes very powerful, and it often seems to have a will of its own. Nowhere better can you see this than with winding river courses.

Surprising amounts

Rain may seem like just a few drops, but can make a large volume.

Try to measure the water that runs off a roof by placing a bucket under a gutter. The gutter of a garage would do just as well.

Put a can out in the open to act as a rain measurer. After a rainstorm look in the can and then look in the bucket.

Could you explain why the bucket has so much more water than the can?

Spongy soil

Pour some water onto a sponge like this until water flows out from the bottom. Notice how long it takes for the water to begin to flow out.

The soil is like a sponge. It soaks up water and releases it slowly to rivers. This is how they keep going even in times of drought.

Rivers of rain

Rivers cut channels in the land that have very special shapes. Many of them have regular sweeping curves called **meanders**. A meandering river is shown in the picture on the right.

You can find out about the way water cuts a channel by filling a tray with **sand**. Raise one end a few centimetres and then pour in water from a pipe or a tap. Soon the sand will have filled with water and a channel will start to form.

Try drawing a new channel shape with your finger. See if you can make the channel obey your wishes.

13

Water's natural power

Running water is very powerful. The energy of a river gets greater the more water there is and the faster it flows.

This is why fast-flowing rivers in flood can carry away trees, trucks and even trains and bridges. Rivers have energy even when they are not flooding. They are able to form valleys by wearing away the rocks over thousands of years.

River drill
In some places the larger pebbles get swirled round and round by the water and they drill holes in the bed. These are called **pot holes**. You can see a pot hole with its pebbles in the front of this picture.

Stoney river
In times of flood the muddy-brown colour of a river hides the large pebbles which are bouncing and rolling along the bed. This is the time they get worn into smooth rounded shapes like the ones shown here.

Waterfalls , rapids, and gorges

When a river plunges down a steep slope, the bouncing pebbles will pick out the weakest rocks and leave the tough once standing out as rapids and waterfalls.

The Yellowstone Gorge and Falls, shown in this picture, have been formed as the Yellowstone river cut through tough rocks that once came from volcanoes. The yellow stone that has been exposed owes its colour to sulphur in the rock.

Carried along

See how suspension works by stirring a handful of garden soil in a clear measuring jar full of water. The water will turn muddy-brown showing the soil is suspended.

Watch what happens as the water settles. The larger pieces, called sand, fall quickly but the smaller pieces, called **clay**, may stay suspended for many hours. These are the pieces normally carried by the river.

Rivers can carry so much fine material that it is impossible to see the bed

A weighty problem

A raindrop may seem as light as a feather, but raindrops add up! Water is heavy. Each litre of water weighs a kilogramme.

As water is so heavy it is a problem when you try to move it, but a heavy liquid can also be useful.

Too much to carry

This boy is carrying a bucket full of water on his head. It is not an easy task because a bucket of water is very heavy.

You can find out how hard the boy's task is by trying it yourself. Get a grown-up to help you and never lift more than is comfortable or you could strain your muscles.

Which part is the hardest, lifting it up, or walking around with the bucket on your head?

Deep pressure

Find out where the water presses hardest by filling a plastic bag with water.

Stand the bag on a table and let the water flow in. The shape of the bag will show you where the water presses hardest against the plastic.

Heavy lakes

When a large amount of water is stored the weight can be enormous.

Water stored behind a dam to make a reservoir may weigh millions of tonnes. The dam has to be very strong to stand up to the weight of the water.

The part of the dam you see is usually not very wide, but the dam gets thicker towards the base. This is because the weight of water is greatest at the bottom of the reservoir.

Many dams, like the Hoover Dam shown here, are curved to make them even stronger.

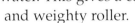

Water rollers

Water can be used to weigh things down and even to roll them flat. This garden roller is filled with water after it has been taken to the garden. It is heavy enough to be useful when full, but when the water is poured out it is light and easy to transport.

Another common use of rolling water is in a rolling pin. Some rolling pins are made of glass with a stopper in one end. When they are needed for rolling out pastry they are filled with cold water. This gives a cool and weighty roller.

Making water work

If you see water spilling over a waterfall and hear it crashing on the rocks below, you will have little doubt that water can be powerful.

Some of the world's largest waterfalls, like the Niagara Falls, can produce enough electric power for a big city.

The problem for science is how to use water power without causing damage to the countryside.

Water mill

People have used the power of running water to work machines for thousands of years.

The power is captured from a river using a wheel. The water falls onto the blades on the wheel, and pushes it around. The turning spindle on the wheel is used to drive machines.

18

Make a waterwheel

You can easily make a waterwheel and see how it works. You just need a circle of stiff cardboard and a meat skewer or knitting needle.

Cut the cardboard as shown and push the skewer or knitting needle through the centre. This will be your drive shaft.

Twist each piece of card until it is bent at an angle and you are ready to try it out.

Use a kitchen tap to give the water. Hold the wheel loosely in your hands as shown and put the wheel under the water. It will spin very fast.

Find the place where the wheel spins most quickly. Is it when the water flows over the outside of the blades or the inside? Does the wheel spin faster if it is just below the tap or a long way below it? Does it still spin if you tilt the needle?

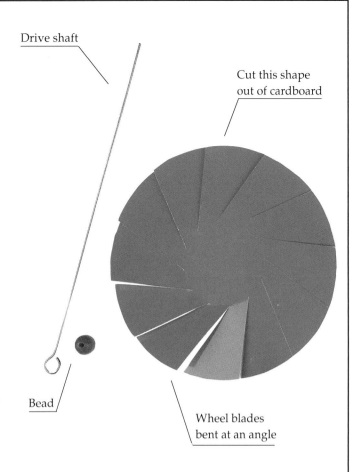

Drive shaft

Cut this shape out of cardboard

Bead

Wheel blades bent at an angle

Power stations

The world's big power stations no longer use open water wheels. Instead water flows through pipes.

There is a special kind of waterwheel in the pipe that looks rather like the model wheel on the opposite page. However, it has many sets of blades and is called a **turbine**. The foaming water downstream of a dam often shows where water is being released from the turbine pipes.

Clear but not clean

You can't judge water by its colour. Water taken from the river or a pond must be cleaned even if it looks good enough to drink. This is because it may contain many small **organisms** or chemicals that you cannot see but which would make you ill.

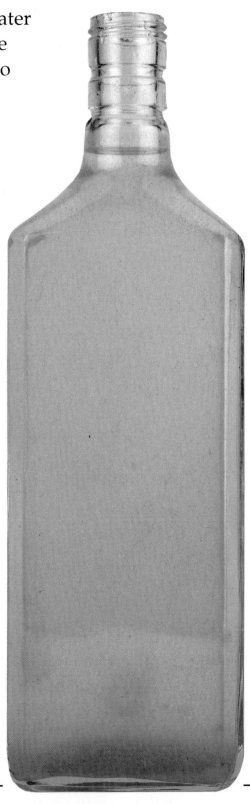

Out of thin air
Treated water is safe to drink, but it must not be left standing in the open air.

Find out what happens to water that is left standing for a few days. Fill a bottle and place it on a window ledge. Notice what happens to the colour and the smell.

Fill another bottle and add a single drop of plant food. Put it beside the first bottle and watch this too.

The changes you see are caused by tiny organisms. Where do you think they have come from?

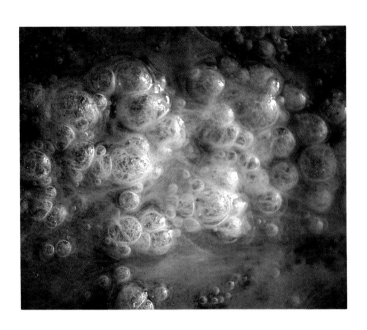

Water for life

All creatures depend on water to live. This includes the tiny ones that you can only see with a microscope.

Some of these **microbes** can cause us harm if we drink them. This is why the water has to be filtered and then treated to kill the organisms before we can use it.

This picture shows the green bubbly slime that forms on the top of some still-water ponds. It has been made by tiny plants called algae.

Cleaning up water

If you took a glass of water and then added some ink, the water would be unsafe to drink. But how would you go about cleaning it?

People put all kinds of harmful and unpleasant things in the water because it is an easy way of getting rid of them. Harmful substances are called **pollutants**. It takes a lot of effort and costs a lot of money to get them out of the water.

Most countries have special places for cleaning water. The water that comes into this **treatment plant** is dirty as you can see in this sample. When it leaves, the water is good enough to drink.

Water on tap

When you turn on a tap water comes gushing out. Have you ever thought how water gets to our taps and why it comes out so quickly? After all, the water-pipes are buried in the ground and the water has to come *up* to get to our taps.

Have you ever thought how people without taps manage?

Pipes galore

City water-pipes can be enormous. The main pipes in New York are big enough to drive a truck through them with ease.

A city water supply uses big pipes to get water from district to district. Then there are smaller branches to carry the water to each street and even smaller branches to each house.

Most pipes have to be buried under the streets so they don't get in the way. Sometimes you see them when they are being mended.

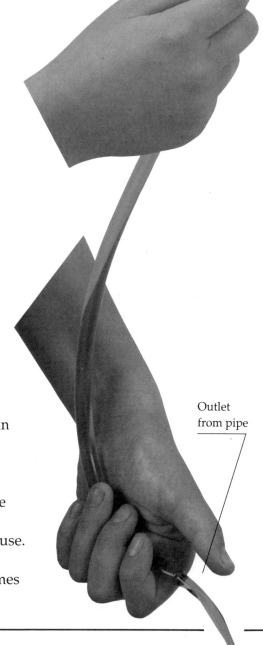

Outlet
from pipe

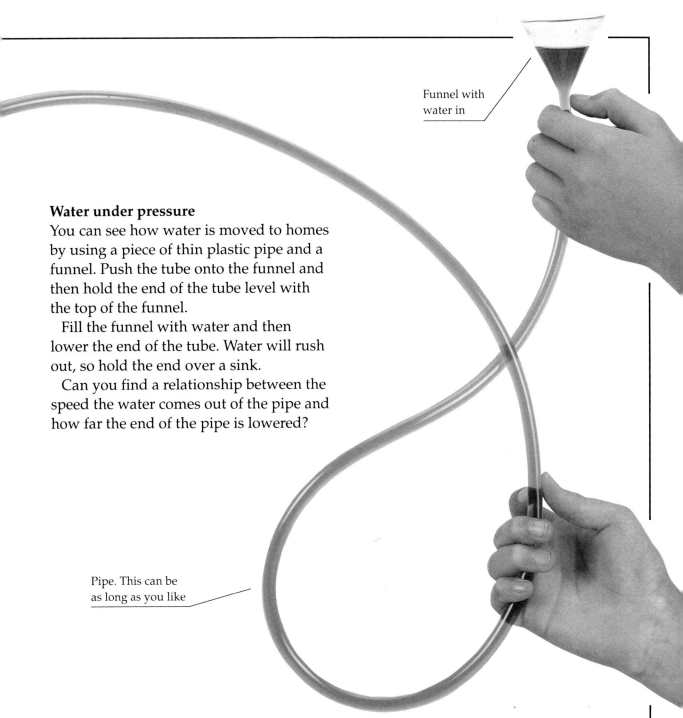

Funnel with water in

Water under pressure

You can see how water is moved to homes by using a piece of thin plastic pipe and a funnel. Push the tube onto the funnel and then hold the end of the tube level with the top of the funnel.

Fill the funnel with water and then lower the end of the tube. Water will rush out, so hold the end over a sink.

Can you find a relationship between the speed the water comes out of the pipe and how far the end of the pipe is lowered?

Pipe. This can be as long as you like

Saving the rain

Not everyone is fortunate enough to get water through a tap. Most people in the world have to get their water in other ways.

In this picture you can see a large concrete barrel that can hold a lot of water. See how a gutter leads from the roof to the top of the barrel. At the bottom of the barrel is a tap to make it easy to use the water.

How much do you use?

We use a large amount of water because we don't have to collect it or carry it.

When people have to go and fetch their own water from a distant tap they use about ten litres a day (about a bucket full and a half).

When it comes at the turn of a tap we use up to thirty times as much.

Surprising result

Who uses the most water in your family? Who uses the most water in your class? It is not an easy question to answer. It needs careful measurements to find out. Here are some ways to work out how much you use in a day and the time you use it.

The best way to make measurements is with a kitchen measuring jug.

To make it amusing you could leave little notebooks around the house asking other members of the family to note down when they used water and how much they used.

Use with care

This African boy has to bring all the family water in barrels on a home-made wheelbarrow. Because collecting water is hard work, his family are very careful in their use of water.

Leave a jug and notebook in each room

Measuring the water used in cooking

Around the home

There are lots of water uses that can be measured. Here are a few ideas. For example, tea and coffee are made with water and so are fizzy drinks. Find out how much liquid your cup holds and then keep a note of how many drinks you have in a day.

Cooking uses quite small amounts of water; washing-up and flushing the toilet use far more. If you have an automatic dishwasher or washing machine, the instruction book will tell you how much water each machine uses.

Ask a grown-up to help you work out safely how much water each of the items in your bathroom uses.

Caution:
Always measure water when it is clean, cold and *before* it is used, not after it has been used.

In the garden

Watering a dry garden uses up a lot of water. Find out how much a watering-can holds, then keep a note of how many cans full of water are used each day.

Drinking a river dry

It would seem impossible to drink the world's mighty rivers dry. Yet this is just what has happened in some parts of the world. Too many people have simply found too many uses for the same source of water and it has run out.

Leafy contrasts
The plant in the picture below is a cactus; it grows in dry places and can survive on very little water. The plant on the left is a tomato. The broad fleshy leaves and the fruits need much water every day. So when farmers want to grow crops in dry areas they need a great deal of water. This often comes from the rivers.

Dry end

It is many years since some rivers flowed to the sea. The people have simply drunk them dry by using too much water.

The pictures above show a way in which home owners could change from keeping a garden which needs sprinklers to keep it fresh to a natural garden using plants that do not need a lot of watering. Can you think of other ways in which people in low rainfall areas could help save water and let their rivers flow again?

Thirsty farmers

When farmers want to use river water for growing their crops many of them use huge spraying machines like the one shown in the picture.

In many areas over three quarters of all water taken from rivers is used for spraying crops.

Floating by

Rivers and seas make useful places for carrying things. But many things besides ships and boats float in water.

Some things, such as leaves, appear to float on the surface, while others, like logs, seem to sink almost below the water.

Water floats on water

Things float if they are lighter than water. Ice is lighter, or less dense, than water by about a tenth. If you place an ice cube in a glass of water you can see the way it floats. Because it is less dense some of the ice cube stays above the water surface.

Look to see how much is below the surface. Float a big ice cube and a small ice cube side by side to see if the big one floats higher or lower than the small one. Can you see if the same proportion of each cube is below the surface?

Danger at sea

Icebergs are like giant floating ice mountains but only one-tenth of their size can be seen above the water. The rest lies hidden below the surface and therefore can be a danger to unwary shipping. Some icebergs are as tall as skyscrapers, and that is just the part above the water.

Pile it high

Look to see how things float by using some pieces of wood all the same shape.

Ask a grown-up to cut about six pieces of wood. Place one in a bowl or glass-sided tank partly filled with water. Put another piece on top and watch what happens.

Stack more pieces on top until you have all the wood floating.

Have you found that the higher something floats, the deeper it settles? Could you check it by measuring after each piece of wood is added?

Cheap journey

Water provides a good means of transport, particularly for people who want to move logs from the forests to the sawmills. The logs are simply rolled into rivers and allowed to float down with the current. When they arrive at the sawmill they are left floating in huge numbers until they are needed.

Secrets of ships

The bottle that will not sink
If you take a bottle and place it bottom down in a bucket of water a strange thing happens. The deeper you push it down the harder it is to push. If you let the bottle go, it bobs up again.

Look carefully and you will see the water in the bucket rise as the bottle is pushed in. The bottle has pushed water out of the way but the water is pushing back.

If you let go of the bottle it will sink only a little way into the water. When it comes to rest it means that the weight of the bottle is matched by the weight of the water that was pushed out of the way.

If you drop a stone into a pond it sinks. If you throw in a piece of wood it floats. It seems that only light things can float.

For thousands of years people made ships from wood because they thought metal ships would sink. But the secret of floating is to use a special shape that keeps the water out. Then you can use whatever material you want.

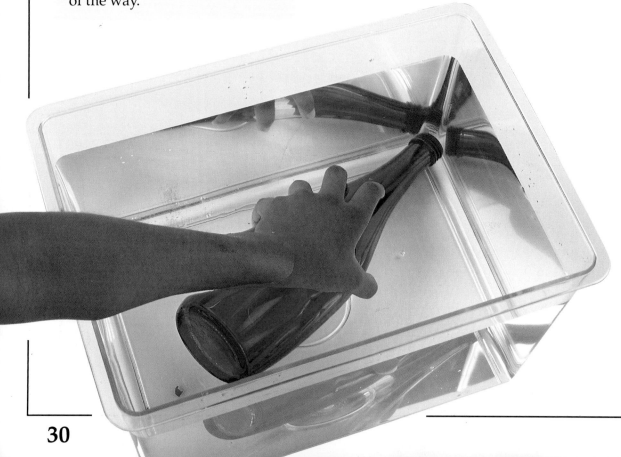

Floating spoon

See if you can make a spoon float on water with only a lump of Plasticine to help you.

You will need to make a shape of a boat from the Plasticine and then use it to float the spoon. Look carefully at this picture for a clue on how to use the Plasticine.

Floating steel

A ship floats just like the bottle even though it is made from steel. The hull is made into a bowl shape so the water cannot flood in. Built this way the weight of the steel is balanced by the push of the water.

This ship weighs tens of thousands of tonnes. And it still floats!

Below the waves

Being able to float or sink in the water has lots of advantages. But being submerged is more difficult than floating.

Nature discovered how to do this millions of years ago. People can now do the same – by using submarines.

Compartments can be filled and emptied

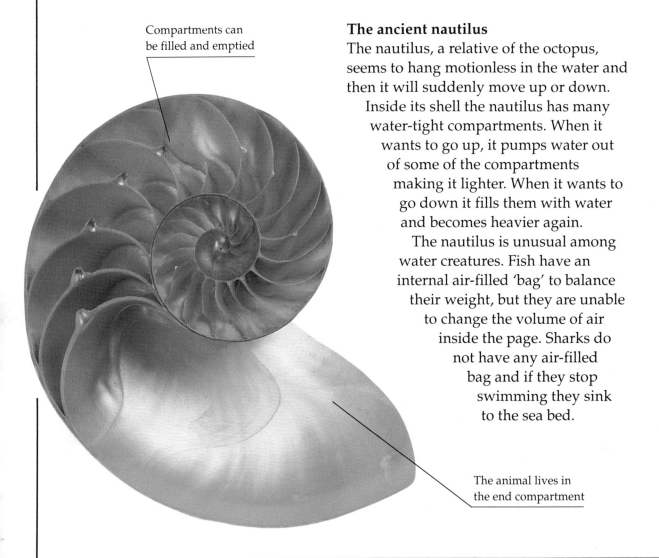

The ancient nautilus

The nautilus, a relative of the octopus, seems to hang motionless in the water and then it will suddenly move up or down.

Inside its shell the nautilus has many water-tight compartments. When it wants to go up, it pumps water out of some of the compartments making it lighter. When it wants to go down it fills them with water and becomes heavier again.

The nautilus is unusual among water creatures. Fish have an internal air-filled 'bag' to balance their weight, but they are unable to change the volume of air inside the page. Sharks do not have any air-filled bag and if they stop swimming they sink to the sea bed.

The animal lives in the end compartment

Submarines

Submarines are tubes of steel built with many chambers that can be emptied and filled much like a nautilus.

The submarine captain uses the chambers to help him make the ship dive or surface. As he dives, the captain begins to flood the chambers. To make the submarine break the surface he has to push water out of the chambers again.

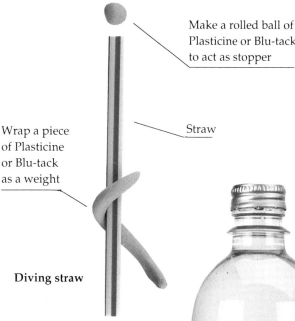

Make a rolled ball of Plasticine or Blu-tack to act as stopper

Straw

Wrap a piece of Plasticine or Blu-tack as a weight

Diving straw

Make a diving straw

Use a clear fizzy drink bottle, a straw about 5 centimetres long, and some Plasticine or Blu-tack. Fill one end of the straw with Plasticine or Blu-tack and then wrap another bit around the straw near the open end to act as a weight. The idea is to make a float.

Try out your diving straw in a bowl. Alter the weight until the float sits upright and about a third sticking out of the water.

Put the straw into a fizzy drink bottle that has been filled right to the top with water. Push the straw down with the screw cap of the bottle.

When you squeeze the bottle the straw will sink. Squeezing puts pressure on the water in the bottle and some water goes into the straw, making it heavier and letting it sink. Submarines use this idea to let water into their outer hull when they want to dive.

Gassy water

Water can take up, or **absorb**, invisible gases from the air. Water creatures can only survive if there is the right amount of oxygen in the water.

Water will also absorb more gas when it is under pressure. Carbon dioxide is added to water under pressure to make our drinks more gassy and fun to drink.

Its a fishy life

Fish have special gills that help them use the oxygen taken up by the water from the air.

In a place where the water is rough and tumbling, such as at rapids or near a beach or a coral reef, the water contains a lot of oxygen. This is the home of fish that need a lot of oxygen to live, such as the Angel Fish shown in this picture.

The still waters of a pond contain much less oxygen and different types of fish live there. If you keep rough-water fish in a fish tank or pond, you have to make sure that the water gets enough air by using an air bubbler or a motorised fountain.

Fizzy water

If you open a bottle of fizzy drink you will suddenly see thousands of bubbles rushing to the surface.

This happens because the manufacturer has pumped carbon dioxide gas into the water before sealing the bottle. Releasing the seal allows a lot of the gas to escape.

Give water a fizzicle
You can see the gases in the
water when a saucepan of
water is boiled. The bubbles
are the gases being released
from the water and then
floating to the surface.

If you watch a boiling
saucepan of water for a while,
you will see that it bubbles
less after a time because there
is less gas left in the water.

When water doesn't mix

Many substances will mix with, or dissolve, in water. A few substances will not. The most common ones are kinds of fat, wax and oil. When these substances are added to water they form lumps or sheets that float on the surface.

Pan filled with water to this level

Layer of grease on the bottom of the pan

Grease test
It is easy to show that water and fat do not mix. Ask a grown-up to leave a frying pan to cool with some fat in it. When the fat has turned white and gone solid and become cold, write your name in the bottom.

Put some water in the frying pan and see if the fat and water mix. Ask a grown-up to warm the frying pan until the fat melts. Look carefully to see what happens.

Oil spill

Occasionally ships have accidents and then thousands of tonnes of oil can spill into the sea causing pollution within hours. The thick black oil soon spreads over the surface of the sea. It will quickly get stuck to birds feathers and can even kill them. It will also stick to the sand and rocks of the shore and make beaches unusable.

This picture shows oil on a penguin. Fortunately this bird could be cleaned by rescuers.

Making water mix

Detergents are special chemicals for making water mix with fats, waxes and oils. Washing-up liquid and the powder used in a washing machine are detergents. Detergents can also be used to help clean up after oil spills.

Watch the way detergents work by filling a glass half full of water. Next, add some cold cooking oil until you have a layer on the surface.

Look carefully at what happens when some drops of washing-up liquid are added and stirred in. The drops break up and become surrounded by the washing up liquid so they can mixed with the water. This is why the water turns cloudy.

Washing-up liquid

Oil

Water

Surface tension

Water will not easily spread out over a dry object, but naturally forms into small droplets. Rain falling on leaves, for example, will form into droplets as this picture shows. Each droplet looks almost as though it is held in place by a skin. The effect is called **surface tension**.

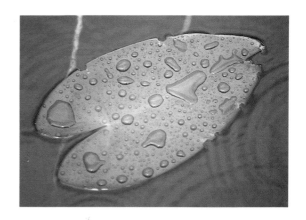

Invisible skin

Surface tension is even strong enough to hold a steel needle.

Try this trick on your friends. Give them a paper clip and ask them to make it float. Then you can show them how to do it. You need a small piece of kitchen towel , a clean paper clip and a small bowl of clean water.

Place the paper clip on the paper and very gently rest paper and clip on the surface of the water. Soon the paper will sink, leaving the clip floating in a small trough of stretched water.

Add a small drop of detergent to the water and see what happens.

Soap bubbles

Soap bubbles are films of soapy water. They are fun to make and they show that water will hold together even when the droplet is just a thin film.

Soap bubble films are made using a wire ring and soapy water. Pull the ring through some soapy water and then blow the film away gently. It will immediately form into a ball and float in the air.

Keeping dry

Sometimes the skin effect of water can be very useful. An umbrella is made out of threads of fabric, but it will still keep you dry in the rain because droplets or rainwater are bigger than the gaps between the threads in the fabric.

Outdoor clothes and umbrellas are often treated with a special waxy liquids called **water repellents**.

Swelling and shrinking

Water changes in volume as it warms up and when it cools down. It increases – it expands – when it heats up and decreases – it contracts – when it cools down.

There is one important exception to this rule: when water freezes it expands. People who use water have to be careful to remember how its volume changes or they can make some expensive mistakes.

Warming up

When water warms it increases in volume. Cold water filled to the top of a glass will take up less space than the same amount of water that is at room temperature.

A bottle of soft drink is nearly all water. The manufacturer has a space left at the top to allow space for the water to expand in a warm room without bursting the bottle.

Expansion tubes

You can see how water expands when it gets warm if you fill a bottle right to the top using water from a refrigerator. Ask a grown-up to make a hole in a cork just big enough to take a plastic straw.

Push the straw a little way into the cork, then fit the cork into the bottle.

Mark the level of the water on the straw. Then stand the bottle in hot water. In a short while you will see the water level rise in the straw.

Liquid rising

Magic growing straws

You need a tough plastic straw and some Plasticine.

Close one end of the straw with Plasticine and stand it upright in a tall flask. Fill the straw right to the top with water that has been cooled in a fridge. Make sure the straw stands upright.

Carefully put the straw and the flask into a freezer and leave it for a couple of hours. When you return an icy column will have grown out of the end of the straw.

Cooling down

Frozen water (ice) needs a tenth more room than *freezing* cold water. This is why a bottle full of water cracks if it is placed in a freezer.

Cap forced off

Shatter lines on bottle

Piece broken away

Making room

Freezing is a very strong process. If ships get trapped in a freezing ocean during winter, the ice can easily crush them.

Even ice that forms on the top of a man-made garden pond can build up enough force to break the sides. To stop the pond sides breaking people often float a large squashy ball on the water.

41

Holding the heat

Water can soak up and hold on to lots of heat. Our drinks stay hot for longer because water can hold the heat. Cars can be cooled by water and houses even heated by sending water round pipes.

Nature also relies on water holding heat. Oceans carry heat from the tropics to help warm the world's cold places and rivers stay running when everything around is frozen over.

Free hot water

Get a black plastic dustbin bag and fill it about a quarter-full of cold water. Tie it securely at the open end with a knot: it should be water-tight.

Spread the dustbin liner out on the ground on a sunny day and leave it for a few hours. The black bag and the water will absorb the Sun's heat. When you come back the water will be much hotter than when you left.

Getting your heat directly from the Sun uses no fossil fuels and causes no pollution. It is environmentally friendly, or 'green' heat.

Solar heating

These houses use solar water heating. The black panels on the roofs contain copper tubes painted black. Water heats up inside the tubes when the sun shines and it is pumped inside the buildings to provide hot water for washing.

Hot rivers

Had you ever wondered how rivers can keep flowing even in a snowy landscape? The answer lies the heat stored in the water. It takes weeks for all the heat to be lost and for rivers finally to freeze over.

Soaking up the heat

Electric kettles have very powerful heating elements. Even so, a kettle takes several minutes just to boil a few cup-fulls of water. This shows how much heat water can absorb.

In some places water gets heated as it flows deep inside the earth's rocks. When it comes to the surface again it can make spectacular hot springs. The water has kept its heat even though it may have travelled thousands of metres from the hot rocks.

Steam driven

If you heat a kettle of water it will eventually boil and release steam. Steam is water that has become a gas. Look at the steam escaping from the kettle and you will see it disappear into the air.

When steam is not allowed to escape it can be made into a powerful source of energy. Most of the world's power stations are driven by steam.

The steam train

One of the most famous uses of steam engines is to drive steam trains. Nearly all of the engine is used as a boiler, the place where the steam is made. The steam is taken from the boiler to cylinders and pistons which drive the wheels.

Making the most of steam power

When water is boiled the steam grows to fill at least 1600 times as much space. But if the steam is trapped it cannot expand naturally and so it builds up tremendous pressures.

Power stations are the world's biggest users of steam. A power station uses steam pressure to rotate the blades of a turbine. The turbine is connected to a motor to make electricity.

Old faithful

Nature can produce steam. This happens when water seeps into rocks that are very hot. Hot rocks are common near to volcanoes.

The water seeps down and fills up cracks in the rocks. Here the water heats up and turns to steam. But the steam cannot escape because of the weight of cold water in the crack.

The steam pressure gets higher and higher until it finally bursts out, throwing the water before it. These hot fountains of steam and water are called **geysers.**

The most famous is in Yellowstone National Park, USA. The geyser, called Old Faithful, shoots up a column of water 30 metres high every 70 minutes.

New words

absorb
to take up a gas or a liquid. Many powders absorb water when they are left open and this causes them to swell

clay
the finest size of rock flour produced when rocks are broken down by the action of the weather. Clay is too small to be seen piece by piece. When moist, clay feels sticky

detergent
a chemical that acts on surface grease to remove it. Many detergents are made of lots of chemicals that can dissolve most forms of dirt and grease

dissolve
the way in which a solid is made into a liquid. Water can dissolve more substances than any other liquid. Many substances are colourless when they have dissolved in water

geyser
a natural fountain of hot water that spurts from underground. The name comes from Geyser, a hot fountain in Iceland. Geysers are found near to places where volcanoes have been active

meanders
the regular twists and turns of a river. Most meanders are formed on the flat land at the bottom of a valley.

microbe
a general name for any organism so small it can only be seen under a microscope

molecule
the smallest possible particles of a substance. Everything around us, including ourselves, is made of molecules

organism
a general name for any plant or animal. The word micro-organism is often used to describe the very large number of unseen living things that exist in water and which have no commonly used name

pollutant
a substance that fouls water. People use the word pollutant to mean the waste chemicals from factories, ships, homes and farms. Together these often spoil water and make it unhealthy and unpleasant

pot hole
pits that have been formed in the bed of a river by the swirling action of water and pebbles. As the pebbles go round and round in the pot hole, so they wear away the sides and also themselves

saline

Anything that has a lot of salt in it is called saline. Usually the word means that the water has so much salt that it is unfit to drink or will harm plants

sand

the smallest pieces of ground up rock that we can still easily see. Sand is commonly found on beaches, but it is also commonly formed as pebbles, bounced along by rivers, knock pieces from each other or from the river bed

solution

The name given to describe the mixture of one substance inside another. A salt solution is made of water and salt, but if the water is boiled away, the salt will reform

surface tension

A special property of liquids which makes the surface of a liquid look and behave as though it had an invisible skin over the surface

treatment plant

A place for processing the polluted waters of rivers or waste-pipes. Treatment works use filters and microbes to get rid of the most poisonous substances. When water leaves a treatment plants it should be good enough to drink

turbine

A machine with many blades that is used to make electricity. Rushing water is used to turn the blades and these in turn cause the shaft of an electric generator to turn. The faster the water flows, the quicker the turbine turns and the more electricity is made

volume

the amount of space taken up by an object. Volume is measured by multiplying together the length, breadth and width of an object

water cycle

The never-ending way in which water moves around the world. People normally think of the cycle as starting in the oceans. They then follow the path of the water through clouds and rain, through rocks and soil, to the rivers that return the water to the sea

water repellent

A substance such as grease that will not dissolve in water. A water repellent painted on to a cloth will not let water get to the fibres. Many raincoats are treated with water repellents

water vapour

The kind of water that occurs as an invisible gas. The amount of water vapour that can be held in the air gets less at lower temperatures, so a cold day forces much vapour to be turned back to water droplets. This gives dew

Index

532

Camdean School

Item no.   00444